ADULT COLORING BOOK

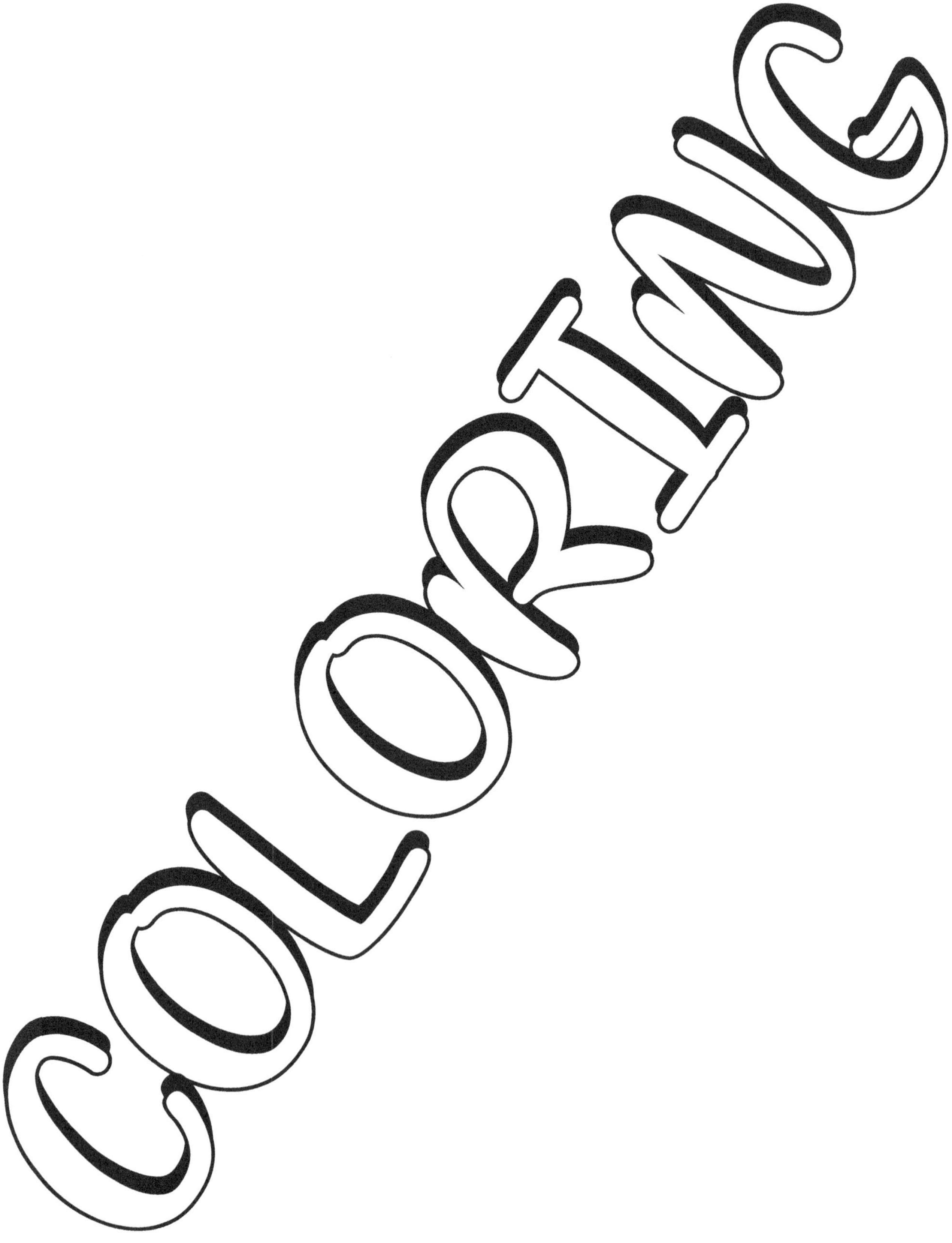
COLORING

DO NOT
MAKE ME
USE MY
VET
VOICE

2

VET
ALL DAY
EVERY DAY

4

WORLD'S
OKAYEST
VET

6

GOD FOUND SOME
OF THE STRONGEST
PEOPLE AND MADE
THEM
VETS

8

5 OUT OF 4
PEOPLE
STRUGGLE TO
BE
VETS

10

BORN
GREAT

12

LOVED

14

EVERY ONE
DESERVES
A
VOICE

16

VET
OFF
DUTY

18

MIGHTY
OWL

20

KISS ME
I'M A
VET

22

I
WORKED
HARD
FOR
THIS
JOB

24

RELAX AM A VET

26

GREAT
WORK

28

BEST
VET
IN THE GALAXY

30

IM THANKFUL FOR
MANY THINGS BUT
MOSTLY FOR BEING
A
VET

32

STRONG

34

I'M PROUD
TO BE A
VET

36

BEST
VET
EVER

38

I'M A VET
TO SAVE TIME
LET'S ASSUME
I'M ALWAYS
RIGHT

40

BLESSED

42

FAVOURED

44

VETS
CHANGE
THE
WORLD

46

INSTANT
VET
JUST ADD
COFFEE

48

BEST
VET
EVER

THANK YOU

Made in the USA
Monee, IL
13 October 2021

79923033R00031